Barrels on the North Quay about 1900. The logo JMP stood for James More, Pulteneytown, one of the most successful curers in the town.

ACKNOWLEDGEMENTS

The Dedication, hard work and enthusiasm of the following have made this book possible.

The Photographers

Alexander Johnston, senior.

William Johnston.

Alexander Johnston, junior.

The Wick Society

Mr Donald Sinclair, Vice-Chairman, who made the prints from the original John-ston negatives.

Mr William Lyall, who selected the negatives and worked closely with Clive Richards, North of Scotland Newspapers Limited.

They were assisted by—

Mrs Jessie Doull, Treasurer.

Mrs Helen Falconer.

Mr Tony Sinclair.

Mr Iain Sutherland, Chairman.

Miss Christa Taylor, Secretary.

and Catherine Weir.

COVER

Top Left: A portrait from the Johnston Studio.
Top right: Gala Procession, Bridge Street, 1938.
Bottom left: Congestion at the Harbour during the 1920s.
Bottom right: Campbells the Bakers advertising a new loaf in Market Square.

Published and Photocomposed by North of Scotland Newspapers, Limited, 42 Union Street, Wick, Caithness, Scotland

Printed by
Highland Printers,
Inverness, Scotland.

PHOTOGRAPHS

ISBN 1 871704 01 4

VINTAGE WICK

A delightful portrait captured in the Johnston Studio, 1912.

Edited and Designed by CLIVE RICHARDS

NORTH OF SCOTLAND NEWSPAPERS, LTD.,

Home of the
John O'Groat Journal and *Caithness Courier*

WICK, CAITHNESS, SCOTLAND.

Pulteney harbour 1865, looking west.

The War Years. Lorne Buildings, Williamson Street 2nd July 1940.

INTRODUCTION

This presentation of photographs from the Johnston Collection is made by North of Scotland Newspapers Ltd., publishers of the "John O'Groat Journal," in conjunction with the Wick Society, custodians of the Johnston negatives, to commemorate and promote the year in which Wick celebrates the passing of four centuries since King James VI of Scotland made it a Royal Burgh in 1589.

The illustrations, which have been selected to cover a wide range of subjects, span nearly one hundred years of the history of Wick, from the 1860s to the 1950s. They were taken by three generations of the Johnston family, Alexander, senior, his son William, and his grandson, Alexander. Between them they took nearly 100,000 photographs and in the process created both a unique record of Wick's history and some of the masterpieces of Scottish photography.

It is especially appropriate that this work has been produced by another great Wick institution, the "John O'Groat Journal," as it has been recording the passing scene for over 150 years. This combination of foresight, experience and above all commitment to Wick's heritage and traditions has produced the volume before you now.

Iain Sutherland,
Chairman,
The Wick Society.

Pulteney Harbour 1868, looking east.

All At Sea

A very early steam drifter passes a sailing drifter about 1902.

A group of skippers showing their beautiful dress ganseys.

Herring gutters and packers in Davidson and Pirie's yard in Rutherford Street, 1900. Most of the workers are from the Western Isles.

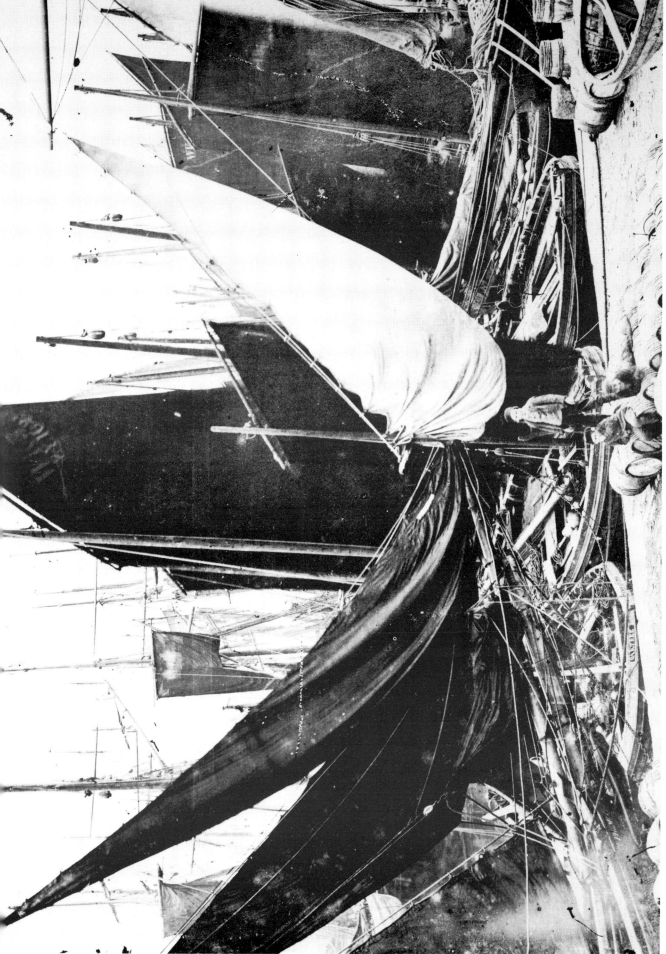

A young boy studies the photographer against a backdrop of sails in the 1890s.

11

Waiting for the tide to enter Pulteneytown harbour about 1910. The foreshore at Scalesburn is in the foreground.

The lifeboat crew in the "John Avins" about 1896. She later overturned in the harbour entrance but without loss of life.

The "Maggie Cook" pushes off with a paddle tug in the background.

The outer harbour about 1905 with the three paddle tugs, which were used to tow the sailing boats in and out, visible in the middle of the harbour. One has twin funnels mounted abeam.

The "St. Nicholas," which plied north and south from Wick for 60 years, framed by the sails of the fleet.

Standing the test of time . . .

Made in Caithness, sold throughout the World.

ICE CHEF Compact freezer with long life built in . . .

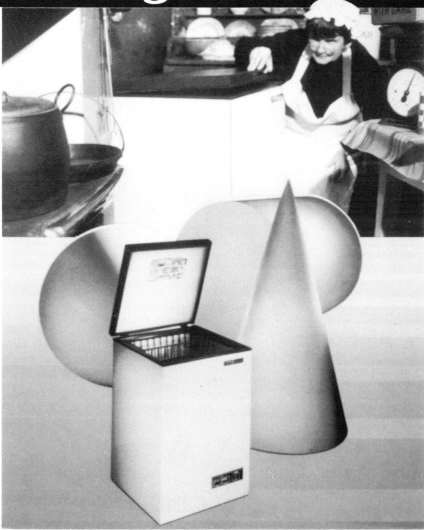

Over a million Icechef freezers have been purchased by satisfied customers in more than a dozen countries, from America to the Far East. High quality components mean long life, low energy consumption and quiet convenience. Safer food storage with the economy of bulk purchasing, is now possible in even the smallest kitchen.

Caithness has long been associated with longevity and technology, from the supply of flag stones for Fleet Street, to the invention of the electric clock.

The Norfrost ICE CHEF continues this tradition of British built excellence, by 'standing the test of time'.

Available from good electrical distributors and electricity board shops.

NORFROST

Norfrost Ltd. Castletown, Caithness, Scotland. Tel. 084-782 333

Heading up and packing barrels in Water's yard at the Camps.

Baskets of every kind in Lower Pulteneytown.

The crew of the Windward line up to have their photographs taken in the river harbour.

A typical scene about 1905 when a mixture of steam and sailing drifters are trying to get to sea.

A view along the Breast of the new harbour before the construction of the wooden wharf, about 1895.

closer view of the slipway beneath the wharf. The Iron Man, or hand capstan for hoisting is clearly visible on the Fifie in the middle distance as is her tiller steering. A Scaffie is hauled on the slip. About 1895.

On a summers evening about 1905.

Barrels in bringing in being unloaded at Scalasburn about 1900

haltigoe about 1900 showing the yards of James More, Pulteneytown, Joe Calder, Davidson's of Leith and the Anglo Russian Curing Company in the distance.

A view in the other direction but this time with the yards tidied away for the weekend, about six o'clock on a summer's afternoon.

The schooner "Flown" arrives back home. One of the fastest ships belonging to Wick, she had a small verse written about her: *Sail on, sail on, Oh noble 'Flown,' catch the 'Kate' and run her down.* The "Kate," which belonged to Marcus MacIvor, coal merchant, was her great rival.

Herring coming ashore in quarter cran baskets in the 1920s.

A congested harbour scene about 1901 with the funnel of a very early steam drifter visible among the forest of masts.

The "Elsie Budge" belonged to Skipper William Budge (photographed about 1928).

Jock MacLeod's yard at the "Camps" about 1935. The herring were gutted and sorted into sizes at a rate of about 40 a minut

The view along the Breast of the outer harbour about 1936. There seems to have been a very good fishing as every boat is landing.

The "Two Boys" just after her launch in 1948.

The "Pilot Us" shortly after her arrival in the town.

The fleet held up by low tide on a summer morning about 1910.

Typical congestion during the 1920s.

27

The "Sprightly" with a steam capstan.

The arrival of the "Content" on 4th July, 1899. She was the first steam drifter to be owned in Scotland.

WK 359 "The Golden Eagle."

The launch of the "Good Hope" by Dan Alexander into the river.

A blockage at the harbour entrance.

One of the masterpieces of the Scottish fishing industry showing the harbour in 1865.

MOVE WITH THE TIMES

The Fishing Industry can depend on our locally based modern Transport Fleet to reach their markets on time

With daily services to Aberdeen, Peterhead, Glasgow, Newhaven, English and Continental Markets. A simple call is all you need for Pick-up and Delivery.

D. STEVEN & SON

FISH HAULAGE SPECIALISTS
HARBOUR QUAY, WICK.

Tel. Wick (0955) 2381/2.
Aberdeen Depot (0224) 898999

SERVICING CAITHNESS SINCE 1925

TURNER & SON

LADIES OUTFITTERS (Established over 70 years)

Stockists of:

HOSIERY by Aristoc, Pretty Polly and Naturana.
LINGERIE by Exquistform, Gossard and Brettles.

Leisurewear, Maternity, Swimwear, Knitwear, Skirts, Dresses, Anoraks, Jackets, Scarves and Gloves.

94–96 HIGH ST., WICK.
Telephone 3187

WE DO MORE THAN PUT THE ICING ON YOUR CAKES

There are certain fashions and traditions in Wedding Cakes known only to the experienced baker.
We pride ourselves on knowing just how to make and decorate this most important of all Festive cake.
With every Bridal Cake we use only the choicest ingredients. The icing and sugar design is performed by our expert confectioner, and then you choose any ornamental or floral decorations you please.

R. G. MacDONALD
THE HOME BAKERY
**97 High Street and
21 Francis Street, Wick**
Tel. 2516

30

Coopers in the Johnston Studio. *circa* **1880.**

Caithness District Council

Caithness District Council extends to the people of Wick their warmest congratulations on the occasion of the four-hundredth anniversary of the granting of the town's Charter as a Royal Burgh.

The history of Wick goes back far further than 400 years but the granting of the Charter was a recognition of the town's importance to the North of Scotland.

This importance remains today in Wick's position as the County town, the seat of local government and the centre of the judiciary. The District Council takes pride in their involvement with Wick and will do everything they can to ensure that the town continues to flourish and prosper in the future.

The Home Fleet at anchor off the bay about 1880.

A typical scene just before the first World War with vessels from many different ports visible.

Another Home Fleet this time about 1905.

Note the size of the battleships in comparison with the fishing boat.

The Swedish barque "Hans" ashore at Broadhaven, 4th May, 1900.

The "St. Nicholas" ashore about 1902.

One of the earliest photographs of wick showing the original Telford Bridge which was replaced in 1877.

Around
The Town

The north end of Bridge Street about 1870.

Another view of the Telford Bridge. Pressure on space was so great that barrels of herring had to be stored as far up river as Bridge Street.

This is probably the earliest of all the Johnston photographs showing the east side of Bridge Street about 1863. This is Gunns Building and Fish Mart. The man with the apron is James Wares, owner of the saddlers shop, and the man with the lum hat in front of the barrow David Gunn, senior, proprietor of the shop. His son, David Gunn junior, is wearing the apron in front of the shop door.

38

High Street looking West about 1938.

High Street 1920s.

Bridge Street decked out for Queen Victoria's Diamond Jubilee.

Back Bridge Street about 1890.

Bridge Street around 1938.

41

The Caledonian Hotel in Bridge Street about 1900, for many years the premier hotel in Wick.

High Street looking west about 1938.

High Street early 1950s.

Bridge Street about 1925.

44

High Street looking east about 1900. The woman (left of foreground) is knitting as she walks.

Another view about 1910.

The fire at George Davidsons about 1930.

Looking west about 1938.

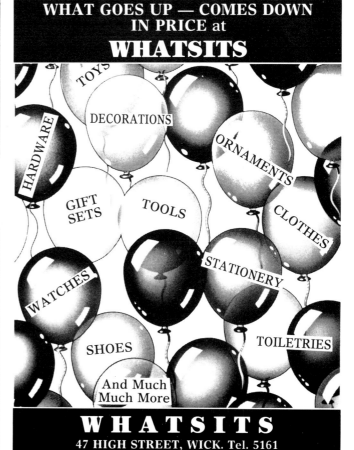

An auction in the Market Square about 1930 being used as it had originally been intended.

Looking east up Dempster Street about 1910.

The Parish Kirk from the Cliff Road.

ancis Street looking north about 1938. The West Church right foreground was demolished and is now the site of Wm Dunnet & Co Ltd.

The junction of Dempster Street and Francis Street flooded by the Luteskerry Burn which runs below the road at this point.

Rosebank House with cattle about 1890. McEwen's furniture factory is visible in the distance.

The 'Ducksie', Grant Street, scene of the famous siege, when police arrested a soldier who had tired of the slaughter of the First World War. The incident took place in the low house on the right hand side.

Bexley Terrace with cattle being herded into a byre about 1910.

The fire at McEwen's furniture yard in 1937.

Looking west on Bank Row past the Lorne Buildings about 1900.

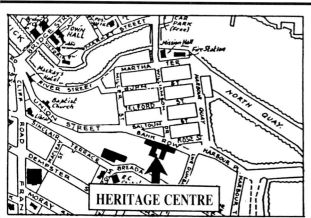

HERITAGE CENTRE

THE WICK HERITAGE CENTRE

The Heritage Centre is the largest in the north of Scotland and has won four national awards for excellence. Within its walls are to be found displays from a harbour with real boats, to a working lighthouse, a radio station, a coastguard station, a cooperage, a kiln, a printing works, a blacksmith shop and six rooms of a restored house with period furniture. The Centre also houses the famous Johnston photographic collection, which covers 117 years of Wick's history, and many examples are always on display. There is also an art gallery containing a broad range of work on local themes.

Behind the centre lie the imaginatively created rose and natural gardens which afford a view across the town, its harbour and bay.

The centre is managed on an entirely voluntary basis by the Wick Society, the town's historic and conservation body, who have gathered all the items, built all the displays and man the complex during opening times. The buildings themselves belong to the Caithness District Council who maintain them and rent them at a nominal sum to the Society. All the design and construction of new buildings has been carried out by the District Council's Special Programmes unit, in close conjunction with the Society, and the end result is an outstanding example of co-operation between bodies, who do not always see eye to eye, but who are prepared to work together with a will on matters on which they both realise the importance to the town and its visitors.

The Centre is open from the end of May to mid-September, each day except Sunday, from 10 a.m. to 12.30 p.m. and 2 p.m. to 5 p.m. Admission is £1.00 and 50p for pensioners and children. Special openings can be arranged at a minimum charge of £15.00 for up to 15 adults and pro-rata thereafter.

Sinclair Terrace and the Library from the Academy Braes about 1920.

Bank Row with the old Pulteneytown police station visible about 1920.

Browns Place about 1900 showing the old South School at the top and the ropeworks.

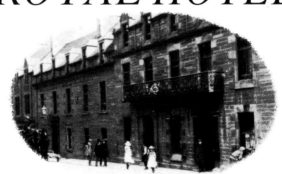

The Service Bridge which was built to allow the passage of traffic while the Telford Bridge was replaced in 1877. In fact it remained in use until 1936.

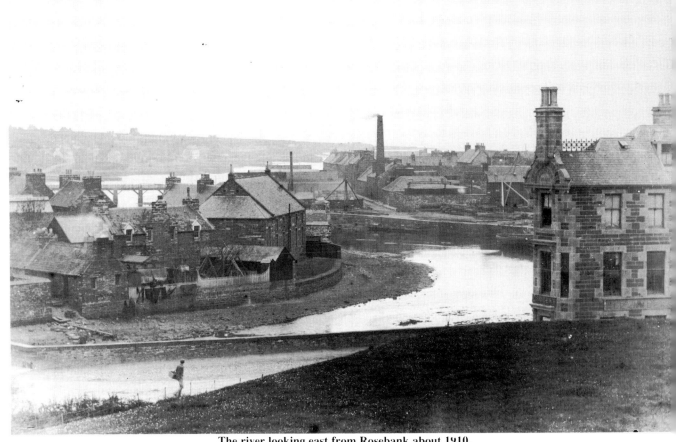

The river looking east from Rosebank about 1910.

Flooding at Alexandra Place, Whitechapel, June 1931.

Another view of the flooding.

From the west just after the riverside had been built up about 1905.

A regatta on the river about 1905.

The Johnstons had both a plumbing and photographic business until 1918. This is their plumbers store at the Riverside.

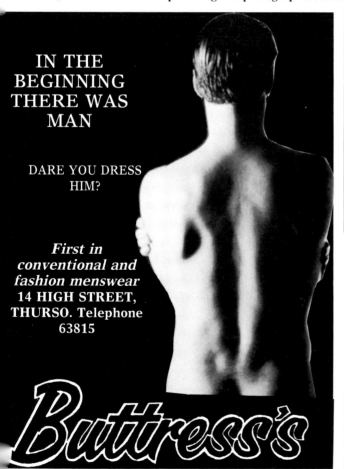
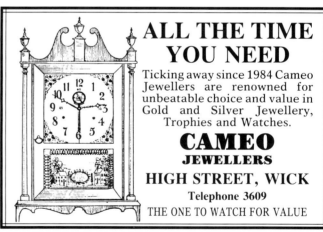

Number 20 Bridge Street.

SON

LATEST STYLES

20

Also on Bridge Street.

LIPTON'S TEA

RSAL TTER

On High Street.

62

In Dempster Street.

At the Camps.

In Nicolson's Buildings, High Street, at the junction of Bridge Street and High Street.

Bridge Street.

High Street.

Bridge Street.

Fashion Specialists
FROM TOP . . .

MARONIQUE

FASHION SPECIALISTS IN
SUITS.   DRESSES.   SKIRTS.
JUMPERS.   BLOUSES.   HATS
ACCESSORIES and BRIDAL WEAR

MARONIQUE
17–19 BRIDGE ST.,
WICK. Tel. 3815

3 SIR GEORGE'S ST.
THURSO. Tel. 65848

...TO TOE
J. GUNN & CO.

FOOTWEAR SPECIALISTS
— in —

LADIES', GENT'S and CHILDREN'S
SHOES, BOOTS and SLIPPERS

J. GUNN & CO.,
17–19 BRIDGE ST.,
WICK.
Tel. 2871

15 HIGH STREET,
THURSO.
Tel. 62712

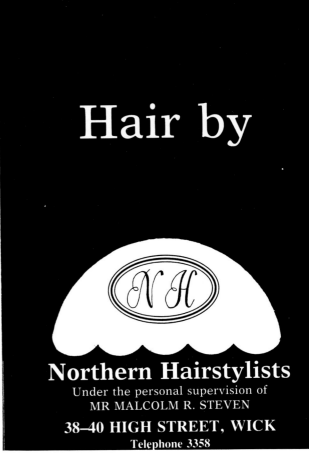

Market Square.

Smith Terrace.

High Street.

Market Square.

High Street.

High Street.

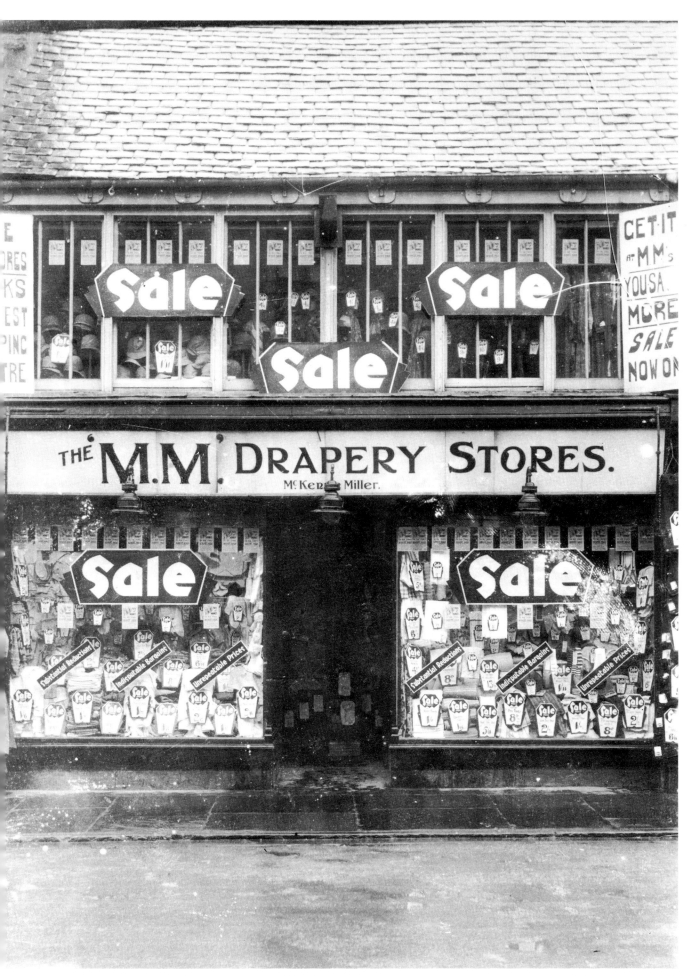

Bridge Street.

A rally by the Bakers Union in the Market Square during the General Strike.

On
The
Move

UNITED
PROTECT.

SK-596

EXCELDA
HANDKERCHIEFS
A NEW FABRIC
ASK YOUR DRAPER OR OUTFITTER
EXCELDA HANDKERCHIEFS
A GOOD AND RELIABLE ARTICLE.

This vehicle has solid wooden wheels.

The three examples of coaches on this page and the page opposite were built by coachbuilders A. & M. Malcolm.

A 7.9 hp Panhard first registered in October 1908.

A mail coach outside the new post office building.

The lorry is registered in Aberdeen so the horses have either come from there or are on their way back.

Carters lined up before the start of a procession about 1910.

Campbells the Bakers in Dempster Street publicising a new loaf in Market Square.

Tom Millers hearse in Francis Street.

ae ambulance presented by Miss Adelaine Florence Henderson to the Police Department of Caithness County Council on 15 October 1927. She also gave £2000 for its upkeep.

Lower Dunbar Street.

In Robertsons Garage at River Lane about 1926. SK46 is a green 8 hp Rover first registered in April 1907, and SK97 is a 15 hp Argyll fi registered in 1909 and belonged to J. J. Robertson, Tarool.

The laundry gets a new van.

The latest Vauxhall of its day.

Early motoring. West Parks House, Newton Road, Wick.

At the bus stance Whitechapel, late 1930s.

A demonstration of firefighting at the Riverside.

J. & G. SUTHERLAND

CRESCENT STREET, HALKIRK. Tel. 208/242

AUSTIN ROVER **FREIGHT ROVER**

70 YEARS SERVICE TO THE MOTOR TRADE
1918–1988

A 1922 AUSTIN PRODUCTION 12

THE EXCITING NEW ROVER 820e

CONTACT US FOR ALL YOUR MOTORING REQUIREMENTS

New Cars and Light Commercial Vehicles. Large selection of Used Cars. Austin/Rovers Unipart spares stockist. Tyres, Batteries, Exhausts, Oils, Anti-Freeze, Accessories — all at competitive prices. B.P. Petrol and Diesel. Full Austin/Rover approved workshop facilities. Electronic engine tuning equipment. MOT Testing. Mechanical and bodywork repairs. Insurance estimates and repairs. Insurance Agency. Self-drive Hire. Hire Purchase and Leasing facilities available.

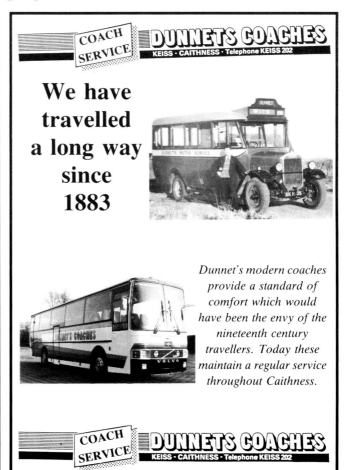

A 3¾ hp Quadrant motorcycle first registerd 13th August 1906.

Topping up at John O'Groats, possibly for a Monte Carlo Rally.

The south train about 1905.

The first train leaving for Lybster....

... and arriving in Lybster at 11.20 on 1st July 1903.

Clearing snow about 1911.

SNOW PLOUGH AT WORK

A pioneer aviator of flight in the north, refuelling at Hillhead about 1928.

A ploughing, possibly at Westerseat.

Down On The Farm

Feeding hens with a haughty duck in the midst, about 1900.

We are the champions.

An agricultural show in the Harmsworth Park about 1912.

A close-up of the same show.

93

Opinion on the location of this beautiful study ranges from Broubster, west of Thurso, to Sarclet, just south of Wick.

This rustic scene was captured in Rutherford Street about 1900.

A golden harvest somewhere in Caithness.

An auction of Clydesdale foals *circa* 1920.

South Head quarry around 1875 provided a large amount of the stone which built Pulteneytown the and harbour.

Trades And Professions

Blacksmiths of the firm of James Macadies in 1883. Their headgear has never gone out of fashion.

Gow's bakers 1886.

Biscuit and pastrymakers about 1885.

Police about 1900.

98

Construction of the new post office in the Market Square. It had previously been in Bridge Street.

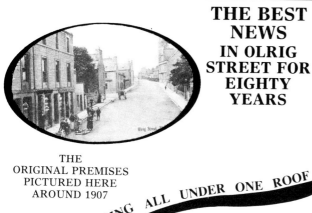

The "Groat" staff at the turn of the century.

Building St. Andrew's Manse in Coronation Street.

The construction of the herring oil plant in 1947.

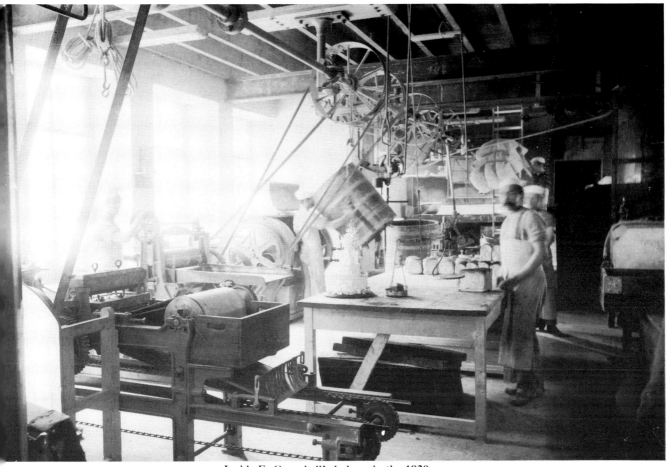

Inside E. Campbell's bakery in the 1920s.

Johnstons plumber workshop about 1910.

The War Memorial is gently lowered into its permanent resting place at the end of Bridge Street.

Ceremonials

Unveiling ceremony of the War Memorial by Field Marshall Lord Horne on 31st October 1923.

The unveiling of the statue to Dr Alexander, the first medical officer in the county.

A garden fete at Rosebank House.

Laying the foundation stone for the Carnegie Library.

The official opening of the Library.

Jim Christie plays to Highlands Dancers in the Market Square, Wick, June 1946.

The Proclamation of George V.

The Spirit of 1941.

Miss H. Manson — Miss 1942.

109

Miss Marie Simpson, Herring Queen in 1952 coming ashore.

Miss Isobel Cormack, Herring Queen in 1939 standing on the deck of the "Sweet Pea".

The arrival of the Herring Queen, Miss Alice Taylor, 1938.

Miss Christine Gunn, Herring Queen in 1953 and her attendants.

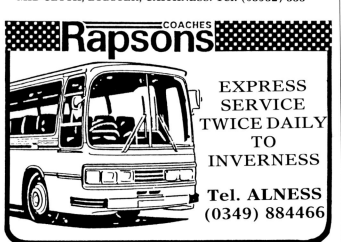

Miss 1940 is Miss Kathleen Davies.

Miss 1939 and her attendants.

Soldiers parading through the town on 6th August, 1914, on their way to war.

On Parade

**Air George Dunbar of Hempriggs and Ackergill
April 1901.**

NCOs of the Wick Home Defence Corps 1915. The famous 'Blin Hunder' and the target of much ribald humour.

The Pipe Band assembled in the Market Square about 1936.

The Lifeboat procession in the Argyle Square. It was always held in the first week of January.

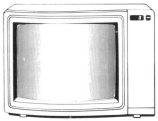

118

Boys Brigade company on its way to the Parish Kirk about 1910.

Another section of the 1937 Herring Queen procession.

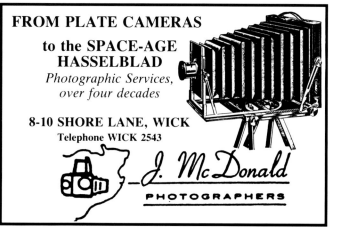

Children's procession on the Coronation Day of King George V.

Youth organisations on parade for the coronation in 1937.

The 1938 Herring Queen procession in Kinnaird Street.

The funeral procession of King Edward VII, May 20, 1910.

Wick and Thurso Pipe Bands leading a Herring Queen procession down Northcote Street.

Wick Girls Pipe Band under Pipe Major Jim Christie late 1940s.

124

A lifeboat procession in the **Argyll Square** *circa* **1919.**

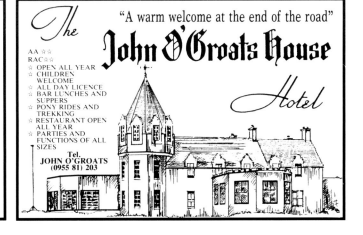

Very early Guide Companies.

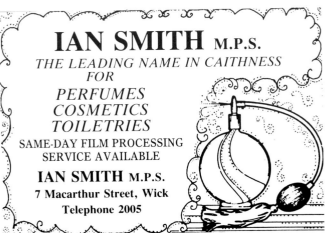

The Wick Boy Scout Pipe Band about 1930 with the famous Pipe Major 'Dada' Davidson on the left of the back row.

Wick Amateur Military Band 1934.
W. Nicol, P. Miller, F. Bremner, G. Snowling, D. Nicol, A. Stephen,
J. Richard, J. Mackenzie, F. Adams, R. Turner, W. H. McDonell, W. Dunnet, D. Rosie, J. Stephen,
D. Farquhar, G. McKenzie, R. Stephen, D. W. Menzies, A. Grant, C. Stephen, H. Mackenzie, J. Mackay.

127

The Town Council 1936.

The provost and magistrates on their way to the Parish Kirk for the kirking of the new council.

The Boys Brigade on parade in Market Square.

Bakers Van in the Market Square.

Floats for the Herring Queen procession outside the Johnston Studio in Market Square.

Horse powered float ready to take part in the Herring Queen procession.

Staxigoe village about 1880; birthplace of the Caithness herring fishing industry.

Village Life

Early Staxigoe.

The magnificient Whaligoe Steps about 1900.

Sarclet about 1900.

Watten in the 1930s.

135

The inhabitants of the Cove at the South Head.

An old boat used as a shed at Ackergill.

Ramsigoe Harbour in Broadhaven about 1880 with cod drying on the quay.

ss Harbour around 1920. Small and handline fishing fleet in the foreground with barge in the background. Note the guiding light on the quayside.

Bank Row, 2nd July 1940, the day following the raid which killed 15 and injured 22 people. Seven children died in the explos.

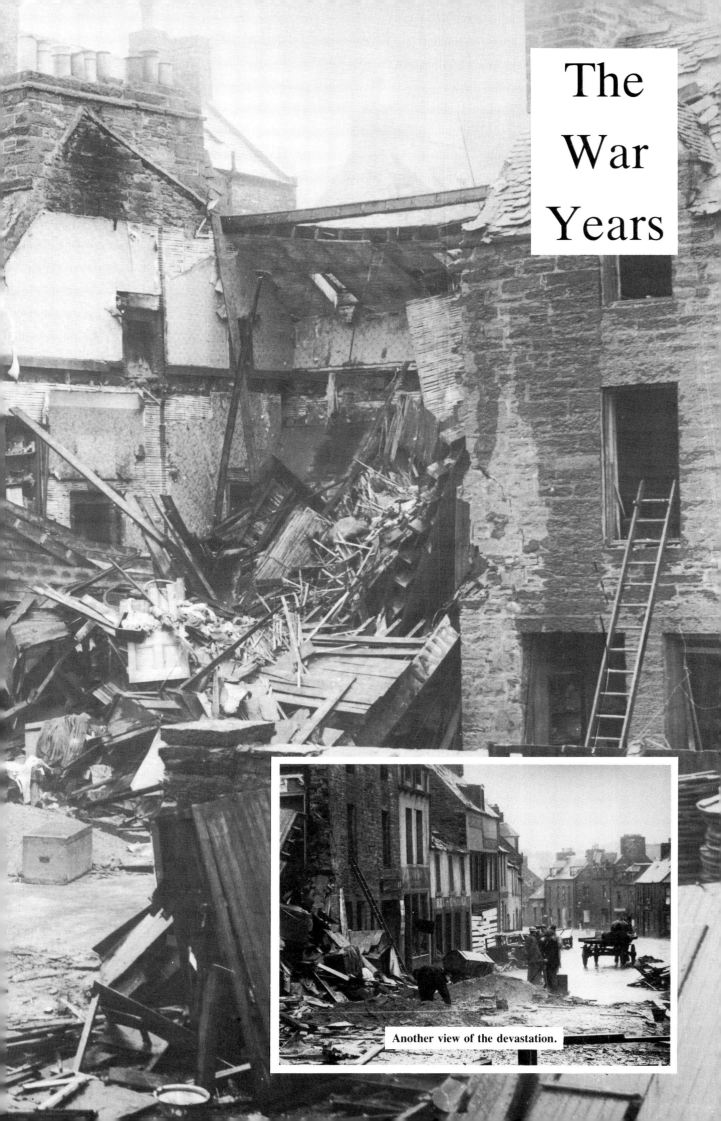

The War Years

Another view of the devastation.

Seamen before their departure to the First World War.

In Warship Week 1942 the people of Caithness subscribed £233,202 and were allowed to adopt the 26-year-old Campbell. All told the people of Caithness raised over £1,000,000 in war bonds.

The Battery at the Coastguard Station used to train all naval reservists in the North of Scotland until about 1930.

Fire fighting practice during the Second World War.

Wimpey construction workers at Castletown Airport 1940 take time out to pose for a group photograph.

More of the "Blin Hunder."

This photograph is self explanatory.

Wick Academy Champions 1938/39.

Sports For All

Members of Wick Lawn Tennis Club about 1900.

At the Trinkie swimming gala 1936.

Members of the South School team in the 1930s.

Cricket around 1890.

Academy School Team 1939.

Tennis about 1905.

Bowls at Rosebank about 1925.

The Trinkie Swimming Pool.

North Bath, the old Blackrock Harbour.

Gala at the riverside.

Possibly the 4th tee at Reiss Golf Course about 1910.

The Health and Strength Club give a demonstration in the Market Square about 1936.

That's Entertainment

Dressed to entertain.

A Freemasons function around 1930.

Miss H. Manson, Keiss (1942), with the famous Mr Jimmy Sinclair on her right. He promoted the new year dances and the selection of queens with great flair and imagination for many years.

A scout dance with Mr Johnny Yuill, the troop leader for many years, in the front row, 5th from the left.

Coronation Ball 1936.

Inside the Pavilion cinema.

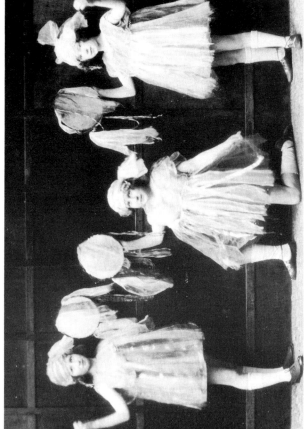

In the Breadalbane cinema.

Pupils of Miss Mabel Morrison, physical instructress, who gave

Wick Players hamming it up about 1930.

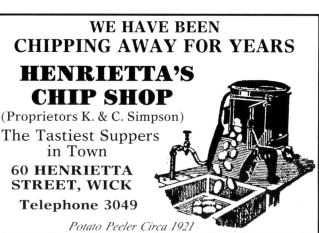

A view of Wick High School.

Opening of the High School, or West Banks School as it was, August 13th 1909.

The South School, Macrae Street, about 1935, with Mr Smith and Miss Flett. It was known as "Fullie's Schollie."

Wick Primary Schools Football Tournament won by Wick North School 1932.

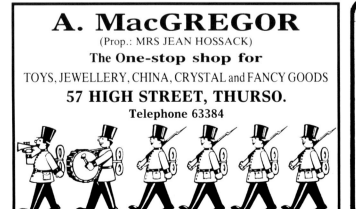

Another class in the South School.

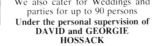

159

The Queen Mother at Wick Airport.

A Royal Visit

One of the Queen Mother's earliest visits to Wick.

About 1900.

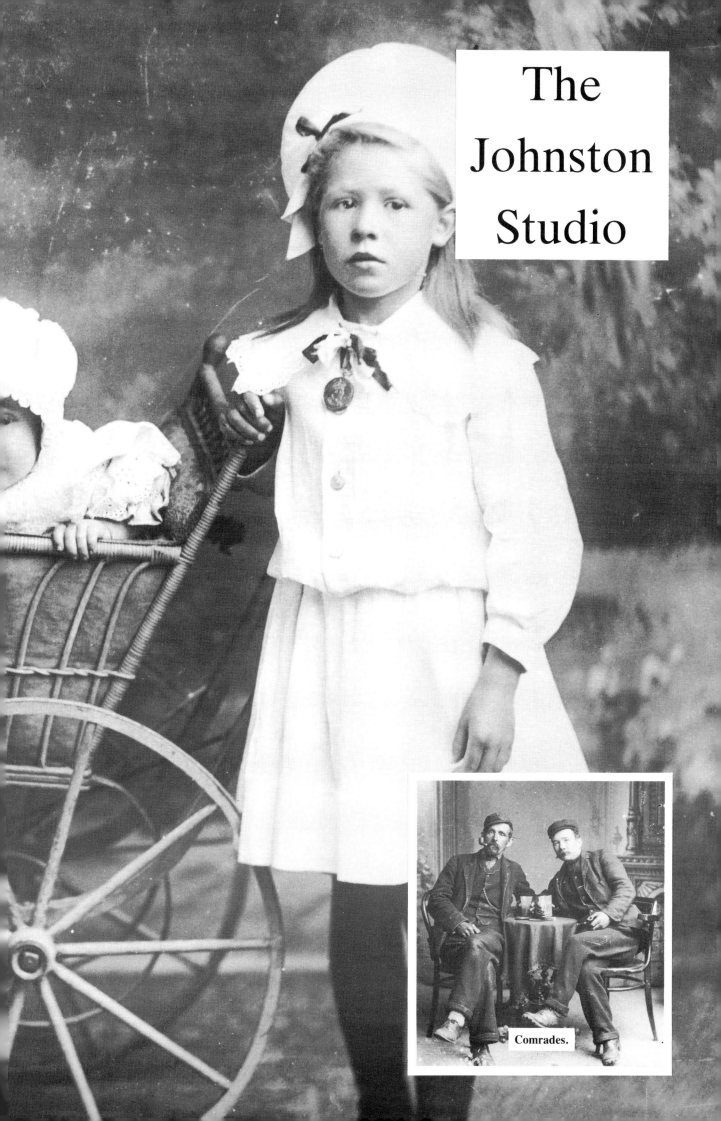

The

Johnston

Studio

Comrades.

Smile please! Captured at the turn of the century

Willie Wagtail a well known "worthy."

Senior citizens around 1910.

A charming portrait around 1910.

Family group about 1915.

About 1905.

Playing with girds.

If you had just taken delivery of your first car, wouldn't you be happy too!